Thomas C. Willadsen

OMG! LOL!
Faith and Laughter

Tom Willadsen is a Presbyterian minister whose writing has appeared in *Presbyterians Today*, *Leadership*, *Visual Parables*, and *Northwestern Magazine*. He is a community columnist for the *Oshkosh Northwestern* and has written a humor column for *The Cresset* for more than fifteen years. His "Front Page News" received the Award of Merit from The Associated Church Press.

Vic,

Keep laughing!

Tom Willadsen

March 2014

First published by GemmaMedia in 2012.

GemmaMedia
230 Commercial Street
Boston, MA 02109 USA

www.gemmamedia.com

Printed in the United States of America

16   15   14   13   6   7

978-1-936846-31-3

Library of Congress Cataloging-in-Publication Data

Willadsen, Thomas C.
    OMG! LOL! : faith and laughter / Thomas C. Willadsen.
        p. cm. — (Gemma open door)
    ISBN 978-1-936846-31-3
  1. Religion—Humor. 2. Christian life—Humor.
3. Laughter—Religious aspects—Christianity. I. Title.
II. Title: Oh my God! Laugh out loud!
    PN6231.R4W53 2012
    818'.607—dc23

                                        2012032142

Cover by Night & Day Design

Inspired by the Irish series of books designed for adult literacy, Gemma Open Door Foundation provides fresh stories, new ideas, and essential resources for young people and adults as they embrace the power of reading and the written word.

Brian Bouldrey
North American Series Editor

GEMMA

Open Door

Martin E. Marty

But I digress. My assigned plot line was very simple: tell potential readers, or actual readers, if there are some, that this book will occasion laughter, enhance their lives, and possibly save their souls, if they have some, and then get out of the way of the author, who has something to say.

A funny thing happened on the way to the keyboard. I assumed that I would be paid by the word, a foolish delusion. No one ever gets paid for a blurb.

Blurbers take it out in trade. They get a copy of the book and a free McDonald's cheeseburger the next time they are in the author's town, which in this case is Oshkosh, Wisconsin. For those who collect town names, Oshkosh is always a winner. We first heard it as children who were not allowed to wear the brand of overalls our farm-kid contemporaries wore. (We were "city-kids," pop. 2,225, presumably too sophisticated to enjoy the badges of farm life.) Evangelical children, farm or city, were not allowed to wear the prized brand: OshKosh B'gosh. It was explained to us that B'gosh was a corruption of "By God," which was technically swearing, and we were not allowed to swear or curse or utter vulgarities, few though they be. (This book has a few which are, I have to confess, relevant and thus legitimate and forgivable.)

But I digress. I have to explain why I am preoccupied with the topic of the book's length. Orders are: insist that Marty keep within a 1,888 word length. I go on like this—almost 300 words already—because the publisher and author stipulate that I dare not transgress by writing a 1,889th word. They evidently fear that a 1,889th word would carry us into *Moby Dick*-length writing. I bring this up because readers should know that this limit induces tension, a distracting fear that I will go over the proper length.

I have not yet written *why* I make so much of this without yet having asserted that this is a good book, not too tasteful but also not too transgressive. I hope it finds a large readership, also among leaders in communities of the sort Willadsen serves: local congregations, since he draws impulse and subjects from them. And they would/should welcome culture-community-church[1] talk, since many oral and written ordinances in such sites are often grim and predictable.

Since I was at least for one academic quarter a university teacher in a class in which Willadsen was accounted for and presumably present, I have followed his trail. While I read his every column

---

[1] Pastor Willadsen is into interfaith-talk, so to be "correct" I should say that "church" can stand for "synagogue," "mosque," "coven," "temple," and other versions of community. (I am aware that these analogues to "church" also count against the 1,888 word limit, even though they appear in a footnote.)

(e.g. in *The Cresset*, where he is a star), I wanted to be sure I'd pick him out of an alumni/ae crowd, something hard to do because there have been so many students through too many years, and facial hair and other disguises confuse the image a teacher carries in his or her mind. I didn't find him in *Wikipedia*, or other illustrated references, but his voice and style are unmistakable, vivid, compelling, valid, and valuable. So now I'd like to help readers locate the Willadsen genre, intention, ethos, and, yes, voice. And I will disappoint him and readers if I do not advance this book with reference to an at least quasi-complex reference. This comes from the late Father Hugo Rahner, brother of the last Father Karl Rahner, who bears an awe-provoking name which by the mere fact of it being uttered gives weight, and the implication of profundity, to a text.

Hugo Rahner, in *Man at Play* (New York: Herder and Herder, 1967, pp. 9, 27) wrote of a certain personality type, "the grave-merry man" (*aneer spoudogeloios*—for those of you who need the original; and, while I am within parentheses I should note that Pastor W. and I both know better than to say 'man' when we mean 'human being' generically, but I am quoting): "Such a man is really always two men in one: he is a man with an easy gaiety of spirit, one might almost say a man of spiritual elegance, a man who feels himself to be living in invincible security; but he is also a man of tragedy, a man of laughter and tears, a man, indeed, of gentle irony, for he sees through the tragically ridiculous masks of the game of life and has taken the measure of the cramping boundaries of our earthly existence."

This is the spirit of the kind of human exemplar which Willadsen in effect commends to readers. Some may feel he is too grim and prim to be a humorist of any sort in these days of *Comedy Central*'s television aspiration and too humorous of any sort in these days when pastors are expected to be grim and dim. Except in the chapter in which he cannot resist telling some churchy jokes, his humor reveals itself mainly in the mere telling of events in parish life and the culture that surrounds it. I'd like to think that church members, some sympathetic pagans around them and in their company, and even those clergy who can pass through the eye of a needle into the Kingdom with enough room to spare that they can read this book will become more like the "grave-merry person" Rahner commends to us.

Let it also be noted that in a spirit of generosity I give back 889 words to the author and publisher who revealed some anxiety that I would go on and force expansion of the book so much that it would have to be re-set and would grow fat and thus cost more, thereby reducing the sales. And that would be a tragedy.

ONE

On the Origin of Interfaith Laughter Night

Planning my community's annual interfaith Thanksgiving gathering brought me some surprises. My hope was that the event would include a wide variety of religious traditions. In Oshkosh, Wisconsin, variety can be hard to find. eighty percent of Wisconsinites are either Lutheran or Roman Catholic. I started by meeting leaders of different faiths for coffee.

First I met Saad at Starbucks. Saad is a member of a small Islamic group in town. We drank our coffee and found that we have *a lot* of things in common. Both of us

> are married,
> drink coffee,
> are in our mid-40s,
> have kids in public schools,
> work too many hours,
> graduated from Big Ten schools,
> grew up in places that start with
>   "P" [Pakistan, Peoria],
> are active in faith communities.

And both of our faith communities bought funeral homes!

My congregation was fortunate to have the money to buy the funeral home that sat next door to our building since 1915. The home was losing business

because they did not have a cremato-
rium on site. The owners built a new,
modern facility on the far side of town,
and my congregation bought the old
building and tore it down. Now we have
"The Green Space" for congregational
events.

Saad's community bought a funeral
home that was underused. It is on a
busy street, across from a high school.
The neighbors were very anxious about
Muslims moving in. The neighbors did
not want to hear car doors slamming.
People who attend funerals do not slam
their car doors, but who knows about
Muslims? The pastor of a church down
the street from the funeral home raised
questions about drainage. In recent
years Oshkosh has suffered several

flash floods; drainage is on everyone's mind. Still, I was baffled by the pastor's idea that this was a reason to block Saad's community from purchasing the funeral home. "Do Muslims drain differently from Christians?" I wondered. There really is no polite way to ask that question.

After spending two hours together, Saad and I headed home to our families. As I was putting on my jacket, I said, "Saad, I've laughed a lot tonight. Are you always this funny?"

"Well, my wife does not think so."

"Neither does mine! There's something else we have in common."

A few days later, I met a Witch for lunch. I had never met a Witch before, though I am pretty sure that my high school English teacher who assigned *Ivanhoe* over Christmas break qualifies. I was not apprehensive about meeting a Witch, but I had my doubts about her religious tradition. Do Witches go to seminary? Are they licensed, accredited, ordained? As we tucked into our quesadillas and started to get to know each other, she said, "We tell jokes about ourselves."

Snap! In that instant, her tradition became authentic to me, and I trusted my new friend. We had a great time meeting each other. Before we returned to our offices, we wrote a joke together.

A Presbyterian minister and a
Witch walk into a bar.

Minister says, "Gimme a brew."
Witch says, "That's *my* line!"

I was puzzled that telling jokes at one's expense validated this religious tradition in my mind. It is not a conclusion that makes obvious sense. As I pondered this idea for the next few days, I came up with some theories. People who can tell jokes at their own expense can see themselves from other perspectives. They understand that to other people their beliefs might seem nutty, and in acknowledging their nuttiness, they allow others to be nutty in their own ways. They are confident in their beliefs, but also tolerant and accepting of the beliefs that others hold. I like to think of this as .38 Special Theology, as those wild-eyed Southern rock star theologians sang in the '80s. People who can take a joke "hold on loosely" to their identity, leaving themselves room to grow.

Being able to laugh at oneself is the best antidote to fanaticism. Usually when religion is in the news, it is because of the actions of individuals who are certain that they are both right and righteous. It is not the sense of righteousness, but the certainty that makes religion dangerous. I'm pretty sure no one ever shouted, "I could be wrong!" before detonating a backpack of explosives in a crowded market or setting fire to a stack of holy books.

As I met leaders of other faith traditions in my town, I started to expect that we would laugh. I realized that laughter was a way to build connections with people. After we had laughed together, we were ready to plan our Thanksgiving festival. Laughter has subtle power to bring people together. Laughter's power can also be used to harm others. Everyone has known the pain of being laughed *at* as opposed to laughed *with*. Ridicule and mocking can be as hurtful as verbal abuse. Humor must be used carefully, even gently. But when used well, humor does *so* much good.

We held our Thanksgiving event at the Grand Opera House in downtown Oshkosh. It is a beautiful building, an architectural gem. The opera house is the only building on the National Register of Historic Places that was once a pornographic movie theatre. (In a small town, one enjoys one's distinction where one can.) Since "the Grand" is owned by the city, it is no one's sacred space. A week before the event, the Grand's community relations staffer called me to ask if he should open the concession stand.

"Wow, I don't know, that's really complicated," I began. "See, I am not sure any priests will be taking part, and since this an interfaith gathering . . . wait, did you say 'confession' or 'concession'?"

"Concession."

We managed to assemble leaders from eleven different faith communities on stage at the Grand, without concessions or confessions.

More than 200 people attended the festival on a night when "wintry mix" was falling. The Thanksgiving festival was the foundation on which Interfaith Laughter Night was built.

TWO

On Humor and Laughter

Humor is a funny thing. Everyone enjoys laughing, and humor is a reliable producer of chuckles, yet humor is very difficult to define. Senses of humor greatly vary. For example, I simply do not find The Three Stooges funny. I watch them and say to myself, "Just put up the damn ladder and don't swing it around so much!" I have friends, trusted people dear to me, who laugh at The Three Stooges until Pepsi comes out their noses.

Everyone has had the experience of missing a punch line, not getting a joke. Once the joke is explained, "Marge, it's funny because the walrus thought she was *pregnant!*" it is just no longer funny. Perhaps E.B. White said it best, "Analyzing humor is like dissecting a frog. Few people are interested, and the frog dies of it." It is best not to look too closely at what makes humor funny.

Most barbs have a target. Jokes usually come at someone's expense. Some verbal humor such as excessive alliteration or rhyming does not harm anyone. For example, "Zack the yak is in the black backpack." is funny without any collateral damage. In most other cases, one finds that someone, or something, is being laughed at.

Laughter is a funny thing. And laughter is much easier to analyze than humor. Laughter can be observed, measured and quantified. The best explanation of the distinction between laughter and humor comes from a brilliant, though unpublished thesis, mine.

Id est, by that I mean "i.e." that is, "that is," it can easily be determined **whether** someone laughed, but it is very difficult to understand **why**.

All my life I have been cracking up at funny things. For more than twenty years, I have used humor in my role as a Presbyterian minister. I enjoy hilarity. I like making people laugh. I have found that people who chuckle together not only work better, but get more satisfaction out of their work. I even enjoy analyzing what makes certain things funny; I explore the phenomenon of laughter. I have dissected many jokes, leaving their remains on the examining table, having prodded and poked their innards well beyond the need of any autopsy. Still, it brings me some satisfaction when I imagine I am doing this in the name of science.

Laughter is involuntary. The idea of involuntary laughter is funny. Sneezes are involuntary, so is blinking. We cannot control when we chuckle, and that can be embarrassing at times. Trying to suppress laughter makes it even harder to stop.

Laughter is communication. Babies laugh before they speak. People are much more likely to giggle in a group than alone. Group laughter can be contagious. Sometimes people laugh with others even when they have missed the punch line. "What's so funny?" "I don't know!"

Laughter is universal. Everyone laughs in the same language. No one learns to laugh. We are born with the ability. We can tell when someone is faking it—even if we've never heard that person laugh before. I'm pretty sure I read this somewhere; maybe I made it up. Anyway, if it is not true it should be.

Once I attended a worship service in Denmark. I had been in the country three days, and I knew three words: "cheese," "exit" and "thanks." During the pastor's sermon, I listened intently for my words, but did not hear them. Several times I recognized "Jesus," thus learning a fourth word. At the very end came "Amen." My cousin introduced his American relative, the Presbyterian minister, to the pastor who had preached. When I shook hands, I said, "I understood two words: 'Jesus' and 'Amen.'" The preacher threw her arms in the air and said with great joy, "You got the point!" We laughed together, in the same language.

God laughs.

Really.

This is a book about Interfaith Laughter Night. I need to bring God into it at some point, right? OK, so read the next chapter. Oh, and thank you for buying this book. I mean it. I have always wanted to write a book. Not really.

What I have *really* wanted is to have a book published. Mom will be so proud. And ten percent of the profits from this book will be donated to Project Open Door, which offers family counseling through the Samaritan Counseling in Oshkosh, Wisconsin. Now you want to buy a lot of copies, don't you? They make great gifts. They fit easily into pockets and purses. This one is less than 10,000 words. [6,381 to go!]

And that remaining ninety percent, the part that authors usually do not mention because, let's face it, it's none of the readers' business, will go to make sure Mom [who is now glowing with pride; you're reading her baby's book!] has the best possible care, the creamiest cream of wheat, the most modern hearing aids, and cable in the institution that awaits her. I promise to visit her there once in a while and let you know how she is doing.

For the record, her name is Marge. Maybe you spotted the foreshadowing earlier in this chapter. Remember that punch line, "Marge, it's funny because the walrus thought she was *pregnant!*"? I was thinking of Mom as I typed "Marge." That is a new comedic device, "the rhetorical punch line." In the same way a rhetorical question does not need an answer, a rhetorical punch line does not need a joke. It is just there. Alone. Alone and funny.

Try it again. "Marge, it's funny because the walrus thought she was *pregnant!*"

Good. Now read that sentence, just that sentence, out loud to someone. I will wait here for you.

Thank you. Now, where were we? Oh, right. God. Next page.

THREE

On Laughter in the Old Testament

Take a look at Psalm 2. The fourth verse in the New Revised Standard Version reads:

> "He who sits in the heavens laughs;
> the Lord has them in derision."

In this case, God laughs at the kings and rulers of the earth who conspire in vain. This is laughter of derision; laughter that comes at someone's expense. Most of the laughter in the Bible is this kind.

Just a few pages before Psalm 2, in Job 39:18 we find, when the ostrich "spreads its plumes aloft, it laughs at the horse and its rider."

The ostrich looks over its shoulder, if ostriches *have* shoulders—someone should check this—and laughs because it can run faster than a horse. Now I admit I am not laughing at this one, but I am not an ostrich. The pregnant walrus on the other hand . . .

Mirth is often contrasted with tears in Scripture. For example, Ecclesiastes 3 reads:

"For everything there is a season,"

[If you're between the ages of thirty-five and seventy, you may add "Turn, turn, turn."]

"and a time for every matter under

heaven: . . . a time to weep, and a time to laugh . . ."

Laughter and tears seem like opposites, but they have a lot in common. Both are forms of involuntary communication [I covered this in the last chapter, right before I started begging you to buy lots of copies of this book], and both are ways we release emotion. Nearly everyone has had the experience of laughing until they have cried. Some have cried until they have laughed. Laughter and tears are how our souls speak. Sometimes the most eloquent way to say something is simply to cry. Still, given the choice, laughter is more fun.

There are some humorous stories in the Old Testament. I can even explain why I find them funny. [I know I risk dissecting the proverbial frog that E.B. White described.] Right after the Israelites escaped Egypt, while Pharaoh's chariots and horses were racing after them, and they were running toward the sea, they turned to Moses and said, "Was it because there were no graves in Egypt that you have taken us away to die in the wilderness?" Imagine a nation making a dramatic dash to freedom, chased by an army, forced to run into the sea, connecting the dots this way: "Moses, buddy! Good idea! You brought us out here because there was not enough dirt to bury our dead bodies. We'll just let Pharoah's army kill us, and we can be buried right here! Good thinking, Moses!" It's gallows humor.

And it is only funny because—you've seen the movie—God tells Moses how to part the water. The escapees cross over on dry ground, and the charioteers and horses drown in the sea. The Israelites spend Exodus 15 praising God, dancing and singing. They get the last laugh. For a while.

Two chapters later, after celebrating God's might in parting the sea and drowning their adversaries, the Israelites are hungry. They complain against Moses, "If only we had died by the hand of the Lord in the land of Egypt, when we sat by fleshpots and ate our fill of bread; for you have brought us out into this wilderness to kill this whole assembly with hunger." Again with the conspiracy theory! How quickly people forget. These people were not sitting around barbecue pits in Egypt eating steak. They were slaves. God heard them crying, knew their suffering, and called Moses to lead them to freedom. But freedom is a scary thing. So is Pharaoh's army; so is thirst; so is hunger; so is the wilderness; so is the unknown.

For years the only Bible passage that I could cite chapter and verse was Proverbs 26:11:

> "Like a dog that returns to its vomit
> is a fool who reverts to his folly."

If you are really looking for humor in the Bible, get about eight good friends together. Drink some stout. I am big believer in stout, the self-fulfilling prophesy of beer. So gather your friends, drink some stout and read the Book of Jonah aloud. Be sure that none of your friends interprets Scripture with strict literalism. Some people believe that Jonah really was swallowed by a big fish, and that he could survive for three days, and blah, blah, blah. The Book of Jonah is not a work of history. It reveals truth about God—and human nature—that is not built on a foundation of fact. The marvel of the story is not that Jonah survived in the belly of the big fish. The great miracle is that Nineveh repented after Jonah spoke only one sentence. Jonah's message saved a city of 120,000 people from God's wrath, and Jonah was angry enough to die because . . . wait for it . . . God was merciful. With the right combination of friends and stout, making sure the reader has a good whiny voice . . . you will be rolling on the floor.

FOUR

On Jesus' Humor

The last words of the Gospel of John are, "there are many other things that Jesus did; if every one of them were written down, I suppose that the world itself could not contain the books that would be written."

I believe one of the things that Jesus did that is not recorded in the Gospels is laugh. Jesus used a lot of humor in his teaching and preaching. He comes across as witty and able to nicely turn a phrase. In conversation, he frequently delighted the crowd and infuriated the powerful. Books have been written about Jesus' humor and rhetorical style. But nowhere in the Bible does it say, "Jesus laughed." Perhaps if we had a record of Jesus laughing we would more easily understand how well he used comedy to show us God's love.

While there is no record of Jesus laughing, there is a story in which he is laughed *at*. The eighth chapter of Luke's gospel shows Jesus having a busy day. He has been teaching and healing, surrounded by hordes, when he returns to find another crowd waiting. A leader of the synagogue, a man named Jairus, is begging Jesus to come to his home because his twelve-year-old daughter is dying. Jesus starts to Jairus's house when a woman in the crowd who had suffered from hemorrhages for twelve years approaches him and touches his robe.

Jesus speaks to her, and she is healed by touching his clothes. Then he continues Jarirus's house. Along the way, he and his disciples learn that the girl has died. Still, Jesus continues to the house. When he arrives, he finds the family sobbing and mourning. He tells them, "Do not weep; for she is not dead but sleeping." They laugh at him, because they know the truth. But Jesus gets the last laugh, so to speak. He speaks to the girl and she gets up.

We may be too familiar with Christ's sayings to grasp their power. For example, Jesus said to the scribes and Pharisees, "You strain out a gnat but swallow a camel." Another time he asks, "How can you say to your neighbor, 'Let me take the speck out of your eye,' while the log is in your own eye?" Clearly Jesus is not speaking literally on these occasions. He is magnificently exaggerating to make a larger point. In both instances, he is trying to get the people listening to him to see their hypocrisy, and humor is his teaching method.

If you have ever watched someone act these two passages out, you would see how wildly out of proportion they are—and, paradoxically, you would clearly see their point.

The funniest part in the Gospels, in my opinion, comes in Mark, Chapter Eight. Like any good joke, you need to understand the setting before the punch line has any power. In the middle of Chapter Six, Jesus performs a miracle by feeding 5,000 people. The story goes that this crowd has been following Jesus. He taught them; it got late; they are in a deserted place. The disciples tell him to send the masses on their way so they can buy food in nearby villages. Jesus tells the disciples to give the people something to eat. They object because of the cost of feeding such a large group. Jesus tells them to look around, and they find five loaves and two fish. The disciples arrange groups of fifty and 100. Jesus looks up to heaven, then blesses God and breaks the loaves. The disciples distribute the food. Everyone eats their fill. There are even leftovers.

One and a half chapters later—it is not clear how much time has passed— Jesus is teaching another flock of people. It has gotten late. Some of these followers have been with him for three days. They are too far from home to return without fainting from hunger. His disciples ask, "How can one feed these people with bread here in the desert?"

In good rabbinical style, Jesus answers their question with a question. "How many loaves do you have?"

"Seven."

The disciples had seen Jesus feed 5,000 people with five loaves and two fish. A week or two later, they face the same situation with a slightly smaller crowd and they ask, "How can one feed these people with bread here in the desert?"

I imagine Jesus asking them how much food they have, waiting for them to recognize the similarity of their situation. Remember what happened then? They do not. The Bible never says "Jesus laughed," but I'm pretty sure at this point he rolled his eyes.

FIVE

On the Birth of Isaac

When I first studied the Bible seriously in seminary, I hoped that I would find hilarious and obscure passages which went like this: ". . . then the Israelites roared with laughter and said unto Moses, 'tell us again the one about the Pharaoh, the serpent and the forty concubines.' Then they smote some Philistines." I found no such passages. I even read all of Leviticus.

[If you ever find yourself in a discussion with someone with vastly more Bible knowledge than you have, you can almost always bluff your way out by saying what you want the Bible to say, then add, "That's in Leviticus." If

you're having a discussion with someone with vastly *less* Bible knowledge, you
might be able to sneak in, "You'll find
that in Psoriasis." Leviticus contains this
gem: "So the rock badger, for though it
chews the cud it has no cloven hoof; it
is unclean to you." (Leviticus 11:5, *The
Modern Language Bible*)]

There is only one story in the Bible in
which laughter is a response to a humorous incongruity: the story of the birth
of Isaac as it is recorded in Genesis 17,
18, and 21. Judaism and Christianity
place our origins in Abraham and Sarah.
And the story of their parenthood begins
when Abraham was ninety-nine years
old and Sarah was ninety.

In Genesis 17, the Lord appears to
Abraham and makes a covenant with

him. Immediately, Abraham falls on his face in an act of worship, an expression of respect. The Lord promises Abraham that he will be the father of many nations, gives the land of Canaan to him and his descendants, makes circumcision a condition of the covenant, and promises that Sarah will have a son. At this last promise, Abraham falls on his face again, this time laughing. The incongruity of two people so advanced in years having a child makes Abraham collapse in glee.

A different account of the foretelling of Isaac's birth appears in Genesis 18. This time Sarah overhears God's promise that she will have a son, and she laughs to herself. The Lord overhears her and asks why she laughed. Sarah denies having laughed, but God insists she did.

Nothing more is said about whether Sarah laughed. God is true to God's word; Sarah has a son three chapters later. She names him Isaac because, God has made laughter for her. The Hebrew name "Yitzhak," "Isaac" in English, is rooted in the Hebrew verb "to laugh."

"And Sarah said, 'Laughter God has made for me, everyone who hears will laugh with me!" [Genesis 21:6, my translation] Let's pause and savor this moment. An elderly, barren woman has given birth. Her husband's destiny as the Father of Nations will be fulfilled through this miraculous, joyous, divine joke.

Immediately, three verses later, we find Isaac's half-brother, Ishmael, "mocking" him. Mocking and laughing are rooted in the same verb. One way to read this is, "And Sarah saw the son of Hagar the Egyptian, which she had borne for Abraham, 'Isaacing'." Sarah was so protective of her Isaac that she could not stand having Abraham's other son anywhere near her. Only Isaac had brought her the joy of laughter; there was no room in the family for "laughter" and "mocking." Sarah orders Abraham to cast out Hagar and Ishmael.

There is a very thin line between chuckling in appreciation of humor and mocking in derision, which is why humor must be used wisely and with kindness. I discuss the use of humor in more depth in the next chapter. Perhaps this thin line is best illustrated by Mel Brooks' explanation of the difference between tragedy and comedy. Brooks believes, "Tragedy is when I cut my finger. Comedy is when you fall into an open sewer and die."

SIX

On Humor in the Pulpit

One of the first sermons I preached was in a small church in southern Illinois. I was a candidate for pastor of a neighboring church. In the Presbyterian tradition, one does not preach before the calling congregation until the end of the interview process. It is typical for nearby churches to host candidates for positions in the immediate area so that the search committee can see the person they are considering "in action."

As I began my sermon, a toddler started to squawk. I was aware of this, but tried not to let it distract me. I raised my voice, but the toddler matched me decibel for decibel. When I was about two thirds of the way through my sermon, the screeching became very distracting. The child's mother rose from her seat and carried the child to the exit. I strayed from my manuscript and said, "I've heard that crying children are like good intentions. They are best carried out."

Halfway through making this quip I thought to myself, "I will *never* do this again." The mother felt bad that her child was misbehaving. The guest preacher, young smart-ass from Chicago, called everyone's attention to her and made a joke at her expense. I am grateful that I learned that lesson early in my career, in a place where I will never preach again.

Until that moment, I had not been aware of the authority and power that preachers have. I certainly did not feel authoritative and powerful. I felt young, inexperienced, and vulnerable. But who else gets to speak for fifteen minutes without being interrupted? Who else presumes to speak for God? Who else speaks from a special piece of elevated furniture, at the focal point of a big room? I misused all that authority to make a joke at a stranger's expense. I knew humor and laughter were power-ful, but I had never used them in such a public, hurtful way before.

I did not set a hard and fast rule for myself about using humor after that. I did, however, realize that the target, the butt of the preacher's joke, must be wisely chosen.

I believe there are only four objects of humor appropriate for a preacher: one's self, the congregation one serves, one's denomination, and the disciples.

Self-deprecation can be a strategy to build comradery and a paradoxical expression of self-confidence. I understand all that, but mainly I laugh at myself because funny things happen to me—and life goes on. Recently a parishioner introduced me to her friend,

"This is Pastor Tom. He's very self-defecating."

"It's true," I replied, "been that way since I was about eighteen months old. It's been years since anyone complimented me on it."

I laugh at the congregation I serve because we always have to have food at any event. We define "Presbyterian" as "Christian with a cookie." This is not a bad thing at all. Some years we use our common fondness for sweets to send packages overseas to soldiers far from home. Other congregations probably send Bibles or inspirational magazines. Not us. They will know we are Christians by our chocolate chips.

Presbyterians are fond of saying, "We do things decently and in order." We have a process for everything. And we make almost all our decisions by committee. It is important that we make decisions after we have allowed people to speak and hear, and allowed the Holy Spirit to move through the people as we speak and hear. It can take us a long time to make decisions because we really value open, clear processes. Several years ago my regional church body was about to vote on a controversial issue. The moderator said it would be a ballot vote, rather than asking the gathered delegates to say, "aye" or "nay," as usual. The assembly requested a vote on whether the coming vote should be on ballots or by voice. We voted for the paper ballot by a narrow margin. Then we voted by a wide margin on the controversial issue. The vote on how to vote was harder fought and more memorable than the vote itself. No Presbyterian would find this remarkable.

When preaching, I have a lot of fun with the disciples. Sometimes I think Jesus picked the twelve densest men in

first-century Palestine to be his followers.
I describe how obtuse they were when
they needed to find food for a crowd . . .
the second time. It was as if they had not
been at Jesus' side as he whipped up a
feast for a multitude. They had seen this
with their own eyes and still asked what
to do. They were as perceptive as twelve
Barney Fifes.

In the ninth chapter of Luke's gospel, Jesus says to his disciples, "'Let these
words sink into your ears: The Son of
Man is going to be betrayed into human
hands.' But they did not understand this
saying . . ."

Until I had children, I did not understand why anyone would say something
like, "Let these words sink into your
ears . . ." Now, I imagine Jesus using The

Dad Voice, making wild eye contact and madly gesturing to guide his words to their destination. Still, the disciples did not understand. Jesus told them repeatedly what awaited him in Jerusalem. Three times in Luke, Jesus tells his disciples what the future holds for him, and they just don't get it.

In Matthew's gospel, Simon identifies Jesus as "the Messiah, the Son of the Living God." Simon gets it. And Jesus gives him a new name, "Peter," or "Rock." As in, "on this Rock I will build my church." In the next breath, Jesus tells his disciples that he is going to Jerusalem and would suffer and be killed there. When Peter starts to rebuke Jesus, Jesus says, "Get behind me, Satan!" Do you feel whiplash here? Peter goes from being The Rock of the Church of Jesus Christ, to being about as smart as a rock in less than a minute.

If the people closest to Jesus—men who gave up their careers to follow him, men who were eyewitnesses to miraculous healings and feasts catered out of meager provisions—did not understand what he was doing and saying, even when he plainly and repeatedly told them, how can anyone today think it is easy to follow Jesus? Here we are, nearly 2,000 years later, in a different culture, speaking different languages, reading stories about him that are unlike any other stories we have ever heard, stories that are supposed to shape our lives, to make us Christ-like, so that we can represent the Son of the Living God in the world, stories in which the main characters are like four sets of Larry, Moe, and Curly. Can anyone imagine this will be easy and straightforward?

It's hard to follow Jesus. Those closest to him struggled. We should expect it to be difficult, too. And we should allow ourselves some margin for error, false starts, missed opportunities, do-overs . . . even grace. Yes, we should extend grace to ourselves. The disciples tried to follow Jesus and repeatedly failed. Can we expect more from ourselves?

SEVEN

On Vulgarity

The last time my brother and I fought, Mom had just answered the phone. Neither my brother nor I have any recollection of what the fight was about nor why a phone call was the signal to resume hostilities. Mom put down the phone and said, "I am so damn mad at you kids!" She charged into the kitchen, pulled the Mirro kitchen timer off the shelf and said, "Fight. I want you to fight for five minutes!" We could not fight, partly because Mom had brilliantly used reverse psychology. Mostly we were terrified because she had dropped "the D bomb." Mom used profanity so rarely that, when she did, it had special punch. Mom knew the power that vulgar words have. Using them too frequently makes them less effective. Using them sparingly and judiciously can give maximum impact to the point one is trying to make. My brother and I have not fought, physically, since 1973.

People are often shocked when clergy use profanity. They should not be; we did not grow up on the "Minister Planet." However, this widespread expectation means that clerical use of profanity has even greater impact, again, when used sparingly and judiciously.

On my third Sunday at the church I currently serve, the lay reader went to the pulpit and read the Old Testament lesson. When she was finished, she picked up the reading and returned to her seat beside me. She noticed that she had extra papers and realized that she had taken my sermon text from the pulpit. She sheepishly handed it to me, embarrassed that she had boosted the pastor's special notes, placed in the pulpit prior to worship.

"What the hell is this?" I whispered.

For the rest of the service I could not make eye contact with her without laughing out loud.

I visited Mary, a member of the church I serve, in the hospital a few years ago. She had broken her leg badly and after surgery was facing both a lengthy rehabilitation process and an extended stay in a nursing home. She had just gotten news of this setback when I stopped into her room.

"Mary, how are you feeling?"

"Well, they tell me the healing isn't going too well, and I'll probably have to go to a nursing home."

"That sucks!"

At this point, Mary's nurse looked up and asked who I was; I look young enough to be one of Mary's grandsons.

"Oh, that's my pastor. Pastor Tom, this is Melanie."

"Hi, Melanie."

Melanie was shocked, *shocked* that Mary's pastor had used the "s" word.

Mary and I simply giggled at Melanie's reaction. Mary and I giggle a lot. Sometimes I phone her just to giggle. We have that effect on each other; it is a blessing to both of us.

Several years ago, I declared that the congregation's Lenten discipline would be laughter. Members were challenged to laugh at least once a day. I handed out cards with the Hebrew word יהבט on one side and its English equivalent "yah, but" on the other. "Yah, but" is verbal punctuation in Wisconsin. We say "yah, but" to introduce a joke or to change topics of conversation. During our Lenten studies, we watched old situation comedies, told jokes, read Jonah and the stories around the birth of Isaac. We even spent a few weeks looking at how Jesus used humor.

I ran into a friend in a public men's room early in Lent that year. He told me that he was surprised that the Presbyterians were making laughter our Lenten discipline. "Lent," he informed me, "is supposed to be a somber, reflective, penitent season."

What followed is the pinnacle of my career as a humorist. [When I turned forty, I became a humorist; at forty-five I became a satirist; before that, I was a smart-ass. If making wise cracks were a martial art, I was about to become a black belt.]

"Yah, but, I tried that shit last year and *hated* it."

My friend laughed so hard he peed on himself.

Now that is judicious use of profanity.

When Mom heard this story, she was proud, in a revolted, tawdry sort of way.

CHAPTER 8

On Interfaith Laughter Night

The first Interfaith Laughter Night was held at the New Moon Café in Oshkosh, Wisconsin on Friday, April 1, 2011. The friendship and comradery that various faith leaders had built the prior fall, preparing for the Interfaith Festival of Gratitude, was in evidence that night. The New Moon was the logical location for this event. It serves both coffee and beer and was the site of most of the original meetings among faith leaders. The owner's band, "Dr. Kickbutt's Orchestra of Death," often appears on stage.

April Fools' Day is a good day for religious leaders to gather to share some hilarity. It was unfortunate that it fell on a Friday during Lent. In Wisconsin, Roman Catholics observe Friday Night Fish Fries with nearly sacramental significance. Jews were at Sabbath services; Muslims had a weekly Friday night prayer service. This left only Presbyterians, Lutherans, Methodists, Eckists, Atheists, Pagans, Buddhists, Quakers, Bahá'is, Seventh Day Adventists, Mormons, Congregationalists, and Baptists.

Sixty people attended and spent over an hour laughing together. It would have been sixty-one, but an Assemblies of God pastor thought the email invitation was an April Fools' joke.

The only rule we made was that one could only tell jokes about one's own faith tradition.

The only exception to the rule was that all Unitarian Universalist jokes were fair game.

Years ago I attended a national ministry conference. At the first plenary session, the gathered church leaders were challenged to "embrace new paradigms! Forget everything you learned in seminary!"

"Done!" I shouted, thus befriending the seminarian on my left. For the rest of the conference I shared wry observations with him.

He said, "You should write these down! No one covers this at Princeton."

For more than ten years, I have been adding to the list of things that clergy learn through on the job training. It reads like 147 fortune cookie messages but with a weaker plot.

One mot is "If you had to shave, it wasn't your day off." A female colleague read this and said it does not apply to her. So I made it, "If you had to shave or put on makeup, it wasn't your day off." Suddenly this bit of advice turned into a straight line. Then I added "If you had to shave *and* put on makeup, consider becoming a Unitarian Universalist." In the words of that brilliant late-twentieth-century philosopher, Homer Simpson, "It's funny because it's true!"

A few weeks before Interfaith Laughter Night I was attending a breakfast for community leaders. I am always seduced by letters that begin "Dear Community Leader," and usually I can cadge breakfast out of the deal. During the Q & A session, another community leader raised a point that was informed by her Quaker heritage. Eureka! There was another faith tradition in town. As soon as the meeting ended, I raced across the room to talk to the Quaker lady. I quickly explained that I was the Presbyterian minister in town. I had organized the interfaith Thanksgiving event, and my next project was Interfaith Laughter Night. She immediately got the concept. She told me The Quaker Joke.

Now to understand The Quaker Joke in all its power and subtlety, you need to understand who the Quaker lady is. She is five feet tall. She only wears sneakers made without sweat shop labor. She has participated in every politically-motivated boycott since Cesar Chavez got conscientious Midwesterners to stop buying grapes from California during the Nixon administration. If she is not your grandmother, she is your grandmother's most irritating friend. This is the woman who told The Quaker Joke thirty seconds after meeting me. Ready?

Quaker walks into a bar. He's dressed like the man on the oatmeal box. Just looking at him, you know he's a Quaker. He orders a beer and sits at the bar.

A young man comes in and spots the Quaker. "Hey, Quaker Boy," he begins, "do some of that funny Quaker talk for me! Call me 'thee' and 'thou.' I love the way you people put 'ths' at the end of your verbs. Talk to me in Quaker, Quaker Boy!"

Quaker ignores him.

The pest keeps it up. For ten minutes, he badgers the Quaker to speak. Then he starts poking him in the ribs. "C'mon, Quaker Boy, talk to me. Say something in that funny Quaker talk you people do!"

Quaker looks straight ahead, sipping his beer.

The young man starts to raise his voice, demanding that the Quaker speak. The bartender is about to intervene when the Quaker finally puts his glass on the bar, turns and says unto the man, "Fuck thee, friend."

I exploded in laughter. When I regained my composure, I said, "You're going on second!"

And she did. Right after I introduced

the concept of the evening and encouraged people to get either coffee or beer, depending on whether they wanted to be alert or to buy the illusion that they are attractive and I am funny. Right after I set the only ground rule for ILN, and explained its only exception, the Quaker lady took the stage, and dropped "the F bomb." Everyone had a great time.

Members of the various traditions took the stage. Here are some of the jokes they told.

An atheist was spending a quiet day fishing when suddenly his boat was attacked by the Loch Ness monster. In one easy flip, the beast tossed him and his boat high into the air. Then it opened its mouth to swallow both.

As the man sailed head over heels, he cried out, "Oh, my God! Help me!"

At once, the ferocious attack scene froze in place, and as the atheist hung in mid-air, a booming voice came down from the clouds, "I thought you didn't believe in Me!"

"Come on God, give me a break!!" the man pleaded. "Two minutes ago I didn't believe in the Loch Ness monster either!"

A late-arriving Roman Catholic, with cod on her breath, told these two:

Two nuns were travelling through Europe in their car. They got to Transylvania and were stopped at a traffic light. Suddenly, a diminutive Dracula jumped onto the hood of their car and scratched the windshield.

"What shall I do?" shouted the first nun.

"Turn on the windshield wipers. That will get rid of this abomination," replied the second.

The nun switched them on, knocking Dracula about, but he held on and loudly hissed at them.

"What shall I do now?" asked the first nun.

"Switch on the windshield washer. I filled it with Holy Water when we stopped in the Vatican," said the second.

Dracula steamed as the water burned his skin, but somehow managed to hang on. He hissed at the nuns even louder.

"Now what?" screamed the first nun.

"Show him your cross!" replied the second.

So the second nun rolled down the window and shouted: "YOU'RE REALLY STARTING TO PISS ME OFF!!!"

In a convent in Ireland, the ninety-eight-year-old Mother Superior lay dying. The nuns gathered around her bed trying to make her last journey comfortable. They tried giving her warm milk to drink, but she refused it.

One of the nuns took the glass back to the kitchen. Then, remembering a bottle of Irish whiskey that came as a gift the previous Christmas, she opened it and poured a generous amount into the warm milk.

Back at Mother Superior's bed, the sisters held the glass to her lips. The frail nun drank a little, then a little more, and before they knew it, she had finished the whole glass down to the last drop. As her eyes brightened, the nuns thought it would be a good opportunity to have one last talk with their spiritual leader.

"Mother," the nuns asked earnestly, "Please give us some of your wisdom before you leave us."

She raised herself up in bed on one elbow, looked at them and said: "Don't sell that cow."

Two Presbyterians walk into a bar, which is surprising. You'd think the second one would have ducked.

A sociologist decided to do an experiment comparing religious traditions. He set a Roman Catholic church, a synagogue, a Lutheran church, and a Presbyterian church on fire. Then he stood across the street from each blaze to see what would happen.

As soon as the priest smelled smoke, he ran to the sacristy and grabbed the consecrated hosts and wine. He was out of the building in forty-five seconds.

As soon as the rabbi smelled smoke, he ran to the sanctuary and broke the lock on the ark that held the scrolls of the Torah, grabbed them and ran from the burning building. It took him less than two minutes.

When the Lutheran pastor smelled smoke, he ran to the kitchen and grabbed

Mrs. Bjornson's recipe for green bean casserole in cream of mushroom soup with Durkee fried onions on top. He was out in about three minutes.

The Presbyterian church burned for a long time. Flames shot through the roof. Ceiling timbers were falling onto the smoldering carpet in the narthex. After forty-five minutes, the pastor wrestled the photocopier through the door.

A "none" told this joke. "Nones" are the fastest growing faith tradition in the United States. These people believe in God, but do not participate in a faith community of any kind.

A man dies and goes to heaven. As he is admitted, he asks if he can speak to the

Virgin Mary. St. Peter says it's an unusual request, but he'll work on it. After many years, St. Peter informs the man that he can speak to Mary. The man is shown into her office and says, "Mary, all my life I've seen images of you in works of art. Sometimes you look frightened, sometimes you look puzzled. I've never seen you depicted as happy while holding baby Jesus. Did the artists get it right?"

Mary thinks for a while and says, "I wanted a girl."

Two Eckists walk into a health food store. That's just what we do. [Manju, the Buddhist priest, pointed out that this joke was funny by being not funny. You could feel the horizons of the assembled Oshkovites expanding.]

A Lutheran congregation was thrown into confusion when their first female pastor arrived. The Men's Club had a tradition of taking the new pastor fishing, but they had never had a female pastor before. They held a special meeting, and after heated discussion and long stretches of moody, Scandinavian silence, they decided to take the new pastor fishing the next Saturday.

At seven a.m. the pastor is in the boat on the lake with Vern and Karl when she looks down and says, "Silly me, I left my tackle box on the dock." She gets out of the boat and walks back across the lake to retrieve her equipment.

Vern turns to Karl and says, "Isn't that just like a woman to forget her gear?"

We even had some collaborative efforts. A Seventh Day Adventist, a Mormon, and a Baptist walk into a bar. They look at each other and say, "What are you doing here?"

Bartender asks, "Shall I pour you gentlemen some research?"

Some clergy are surprised to find each other in hell.

The Presbyterian minister asks the Episcopal priest, "What did you do to end up here?"

"They got me on two counts: I passed the salt and not the pepper. Then I served red wine with fish. What about you?"

"After the fire inspector came through our building, he told us we needed a fire extinguisher for the kitchen. So I bought one and mounted it on the wall, without consulting the Buildings and Grounds Committee."

The Unitarian Universalist minister said, "On my last Sunday before retiring, I took a clear, undeniable stand against something."

"What?" they all asked.

"Murder."

The Lutheran pastor said that at a regional gathering, she had mentioned that attendance was up slightly in her congregation.

The Zen Monk was there because he clapped with both hands.

The assembled faith leaders ran out of

jokes. Besides, we had to clear the bar for the drag show that was about to start, so the Bahá'is were invited onto stage. We closed the evening with a rousing chorus of "The Bahá'i Song" sung to the tune of the Beach Boys' hit "Barbara Ann."

Open a bottle of stout, invite your friends, and sing along!

New lyrics by Tom Willadsen & Jeff Balch

Ba ba ba, ba ba bahá'i
Ba ba ba, ba ba bahá'i
Ba ba ba, ba ba bahá'i
We got Allah and Jehovah,
Jesus and the Buddha oh, Bahá'i
Ba ba ba, ba ba bahá'i

Tried to be Hindu,
Maybe I'm a Jew
Tried to be Hindu,
But I knew it wouldn't do!
Oh Bahá'i, ba ba bahái
You got me kvetchin' and a-noshin'
Leavin' Land o' Goshen!
Ba ba ba, ba ba bahá'i

In Sunday school
I was pretty cool
Normal Baptist guy but
I thought I'd try Ba'há'i
Oh Ba'hái
Ba ba ba, ba ba bahá'i
We got Allah and Jehovah,
Jesus and the Buddha oh Bahá'i!